DAD, PLEASE TELL ME YOUR STORY.

A Father's Guided Life Story Journal For Sharing His Memories.

With Love, To:

_____

From:

_____

You've lived a life full of fascinating details and life lessons
that creates a unique history for your family
and future generations.

This journal offers thought-provoking prompts for all stages
of life. As you record your life lessons, experiences,
memories, and wisdom in this journal, you are creating a
timeless treasure for your children and future generations.

Please feel free to write from your heart and work through
the prompts and questions at your own pace. Enjoy your
journey down memory lane as you write your life story.

Attach a current picture here.

Family Tree

BIRTH AND CHILDHOOD

Full Name:

Birth Date:

Day of the week: Time:

Place of birth:

Weight: Length:

Eyes Color:

Hair Color:

BirthMarks:

Your Baby Photo.

What is the story about your name?

_____

_____

_____

_____

How did your parents and family describe you as a baby? What story was shared about your birth?

_____

_____

_____

_____

_____

_____

_____

_____

_____

_____

_____

_____

_____

What were your first words? When did you take your first steps?

_____

_____

_____

WHAT WAS HAPPENING DURING THE
YEAR OF YOUR BIRTH?

(Tip: The answers to the questions below can be found on the internet)

Top Song: _____

Best Movie: _____

Best Actor: _____

Best Actress: _____

Top Toy/s: _____

Top Book: _____

WHAT WERE THE PRICES OF:

Loaf of bread: _____

1 dozen eggs: _____

Milk: _____

New car: _____

A gallon of gas: _____

Average Income: _____

Minimum Wage: _____

HISTORICAL EVENTS:

_____

_____

_____

_____

_____

_____

_____

_____

_____

Where did you grow up? What was your neighbourhood like? Describe your childhood home?

_____

_____

_____

_____

_____

_____

_____

_____

_____

_____

_____

_____

_____

_____

_____

_____

_____

_____

_____

_____

Growing up, what kind of games did you enjoy playing? What were your favourite toys as a child?

_____

_____

_____

_____

_____

_____

_____

_____

_____

What pets did you have growing up? What were their names?

_____

_____

_____

_____

_____

_____

_____

_____

_____

Which kind of books did you enjoy reading?
Which authors or books were your favorites? What was
your favorite bedtime story?

As a child, did you collect anything?
What were your hobbies?

_____

_____

_____

_____

_____

_____

_____

_____

_____

_____

_____

_____

_____

_____

_____

_____

_____

_____

_____

_____

_____

_____

Who was your best friend as a child?
Describe your friendship?

_____

_____

_____

_____

_____

_____

_____

_____

_____

_____

_____

_____

_____

_____

_____

_____

_____

_____

_____

_____

_____

What kind of chores did you do as a child?
If you received an allowance, how did you spend it?
Which chores did you not enjoy?

_____

_____

_____

_____

_____

_____

_____

_____

_____

_____

_____

_____

_____

_____

_____

_____

_____

_____

_____

_____

As a child, what did you want to be?

_____

_____

_____

_____

_____

_____

Describe a typical day during your childhood?

_____

_____

_____

_____

_____

_____

_____

_____

_____

_____

_____

_____

_____

What was your nickname and why?

_____

_____

_____

_____

_____

What did you do when you were bored?

_____

_____

_____

_____

_____

_____

_____

_____

_____

_____

_____

_____

_____

Where did you go to school? What were your favourite lessons? Have you won an award while at school? What was it for?

What are some things you miss about being a child?
Looking back, what were you like as a child?
What were you good at?

_____

_____

_____

_____

_____

_____

_____

_____

_____

_____

_____

_____

_____

_____

_____

_____

_____

_____

_____

_____

Describe a few present-day things that remind you of your childhood?

_____

_____

_____

_____

_____

_____

_____

_____

_____

_____

_____

_____

_____

_____

_____

_____

_____

_____

_____

_____

_____

Describe some of your favourite childhood memories?

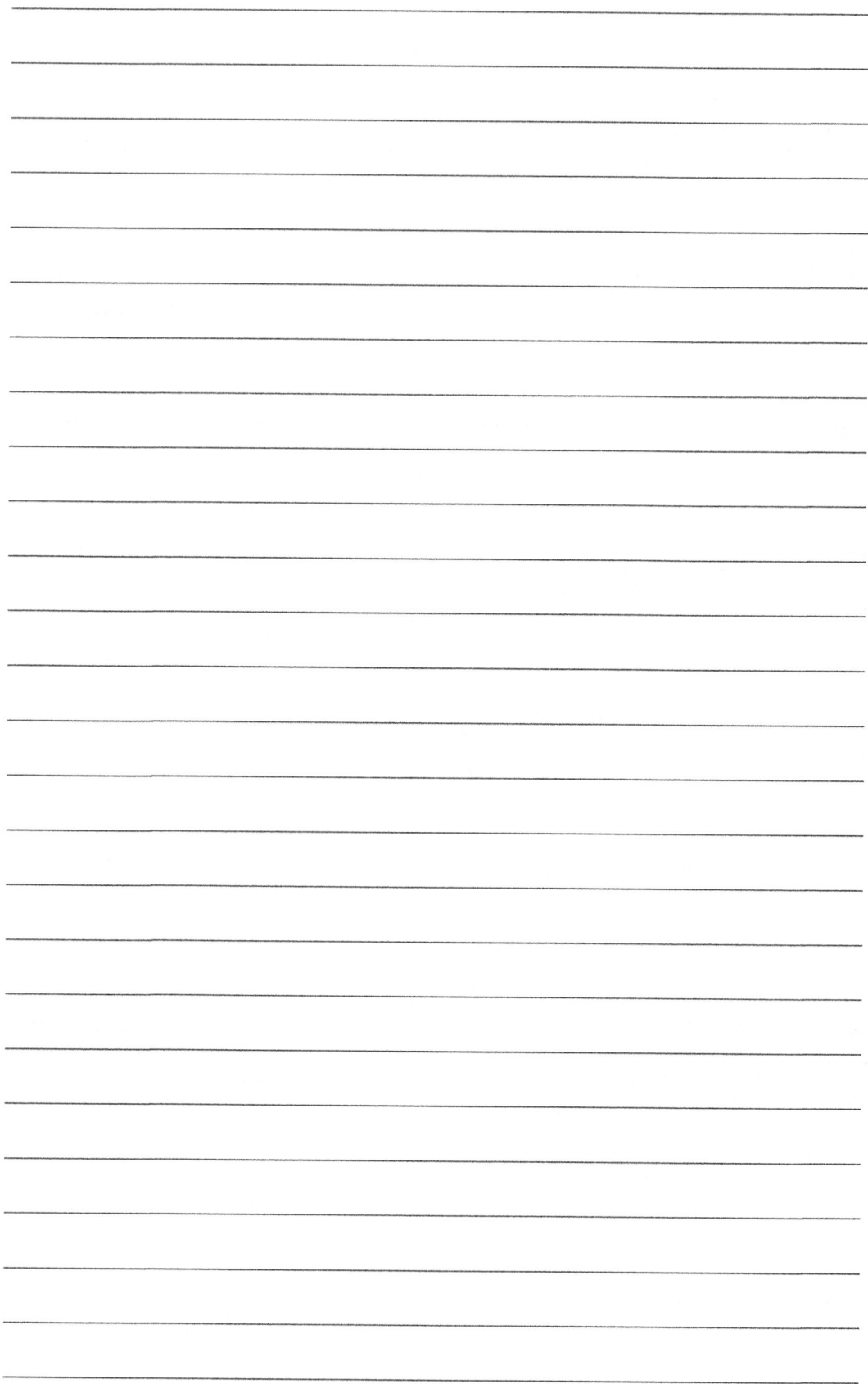

TEENAGER

When you were a teenager, which school did you attend?
What were your favorite/least favorite classes in school?

_____

_____

_____

_____

_____

_____

_____

How did you feel about school?
What was a typical school day for you as a teen?

_____

_____

_____

_____

_____

_____

_____

_____

_____

When you were a teenager, who were your best friends? What are some memories you have of them?

_____

_____

_____

_____

_____

_____

_____

_____

_____

_____

_____

_____

_____

_____

_____

_____

_____

_____

How would you describe your mother and father?
Describe their personalities, hobbies, values,
and what they were good at.

Mother Full Name:
_____

Place/Date of birth:
_____

_____

_____

_____

_____

_____

_____

_____

_____

_____

_____

_____

_____

_____

_____

_____

_____

_____

_____

_____

Father Full Name:

Place/Date of birth:

What did your parents do for work?

_____

_____

_____

_____

_____

_____

_____

_____

What do you have in common with your parents?

_____

_____

_____

_____

_____

_____

_____

_____

_____

How would you describe your grandparents?

When you were a teenager, how did you spend your weekends?

_____

_____

_____

_____

_____

_____

_____

_____

_____

_____

_____

_____

_____

_____

_____

_____

_____

_____

_____

When you were a teenager, what kind of music did you listen to? Who were your favorite singers?

_____

_____

_____

_____

_____

_____

_____

_____

_____

_____

_____

_____

_____

_____

_____

_____

_____

_____

_____

How did you spend your afternoons after school?

_____

_____

_____

_____

_____

_____

_____

_____

_____

Do you remember your first crush? Did he/she like you too?

_____

_____

_____

_____

_____

_____

_____

_____

_____

Have you ever experienced heartbreak in your teen years? What caused it and how did you deal with it?

_____

_____

_____

_____

_____

_____

_____

_____

_____

_____

_____

_____

_____

_____

_____

_____

_____

_____

_____

_____

_____

_____

What did you wear to your first (school) dance? Share some memorable moments?

_____

_____

_____

_____

_____

_____

_____

_____

_____

_____

_____

_____

_____

_____

_____

_____

_____

_____

_____

_____

What are some of the fears you had as a teenager?

What were your hobbies as a teen?

_____

_____

_____

_____

_____

_____

_____

_____

_____

As a teen, was there anything you treasured? Why?

_____

_____

_____

_____

_____

_____

_____

_____

_____

What was the most difficult part of
your childhood as a teen?

_____

_____

_____

_____

_____

_____

_____

_____

_____

_____

_____

_____

_____

_____

_____

_____

_____

_____

_____

_____

_____

_____

What would your high school/teen friends say about you?

_____

_____

_____

_____

_____

_____

_____

_____

_____

_____

_____

_____

_____

_____

_____

_____

_____

_____

_____

As a teen, who inspired you the most? Why?

TEEN FAVORITES

What was/were your favourite:

Movie/s:
_____

_____

_____

_____

_____

Song/s:
_____

_____

_____

_____

_____

Actor/Actress:
_____

_____

_____

_____

_____

Meal/s:
_____

_____

_____

_____

_____

During your teenage years, what did you want to be one day? What or who influenced your choice?

_____

_____

_____

_____

_____

_____

_____

_____

_____

_____

_____

_____

_____

_____

_____

_____

_____

_____

_____

_____

_____

SIBLINGS

Name:

Date of Birth:

Place of Birth:

Personality and other details:

_____

_____

_____

_____

_____

Name:

Date of Birth:

Place of Birth:

Personality and other details:

_____

_____

_____

_____

_____

Name:

Date of Birth:

Place of Birth:

Personality and other details:

_____

_____

_____

_____

SIBLINGS

Name:

Date of Birth:

Place of Birth:

Personality and other details:

_____

_____

_____

_____

_____

Name:

Date of Birth:

Place of Birth:

Personality and other details:

_____

_____

_____

_____

Name:

Date of Birth:

Place of Birth:

Personality and other details:

_____

_____

_____

Share some of your favourite teen memories?

What would you describe as a typical home meal from your childhood? Did you eat meals together as a family? How were mealtimes?

_____

_____

_____

_____

_____

_____

_____

_____

_____

_____

_____

_____

_____

_____

_____

_____

_____

_____

_____

_____

_____

_____

What was your family's favorite holiday? Explain why. When was it celebrated? What is a memorable moment from one of those holidays?

_____

_____

_____

_____

_____

_____

_____

_____

_____

_____

_____

_____

_____

_____

_____

_____

_____

_____

_____

_____

_____

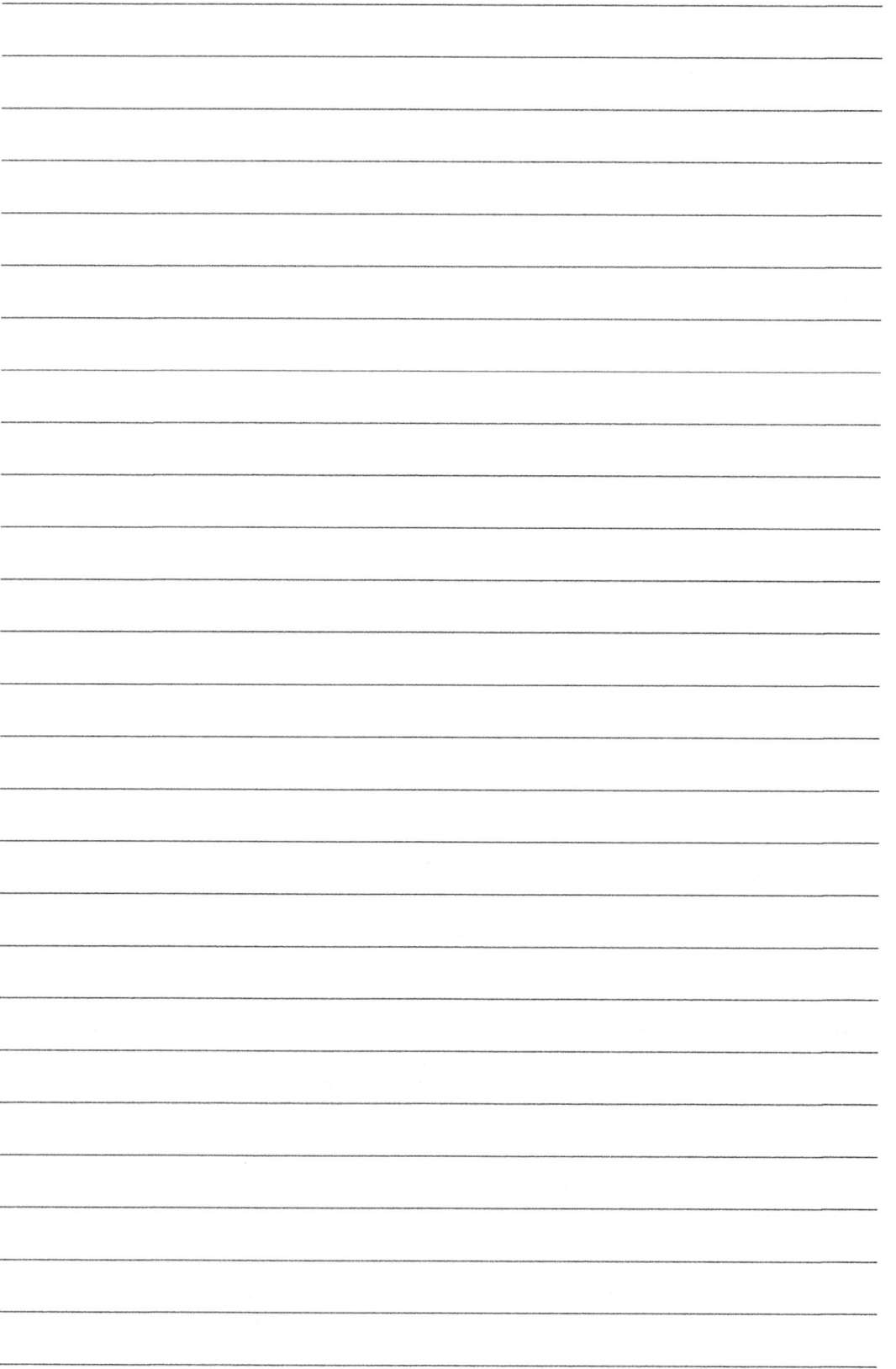

Describe your earliest childhood memory? What makes it so memorable to you?

_____

_____

_____

_____

_____

_____

_____

_____

_____

_____

_____

_____

_____

_____

_____

_____

_____

_____

_____

_____

_____

_____

_____

During your childhood, what was the most frightening thing to you?

_____

_____

_____

_____

_____

_____

_____

_____

_____

_____

_____

_____

_____

_____

_____

_____

_____

_____

_____

_____

_____

_____

_____

_____

What are the events and accomplishments from your childhood that mean most to you?

_____

_____

_____

_____

_____

_____

_____

_____

_____

_____

_____

_____

_____

_____

_____

_____

_____

_____

_____

_____

Have your parents' tastes and interests influenced you in any way? If so, how?

_____

_____

_____

_____

_____

_____

_____

_____

_____

_____

_____

_____

_____

_____

_____

_____

_____

_____

_____

_____

_____

_____

_____

_____

Growing up, what stories did you hear about your family's heritage and background?

_____

_____

_____

_____

_____

_____

_____

_____

_____

_____

_____

_____

_____

_____

_____

_____

_____

_____

_____

_____

_____

_____

_____

_____

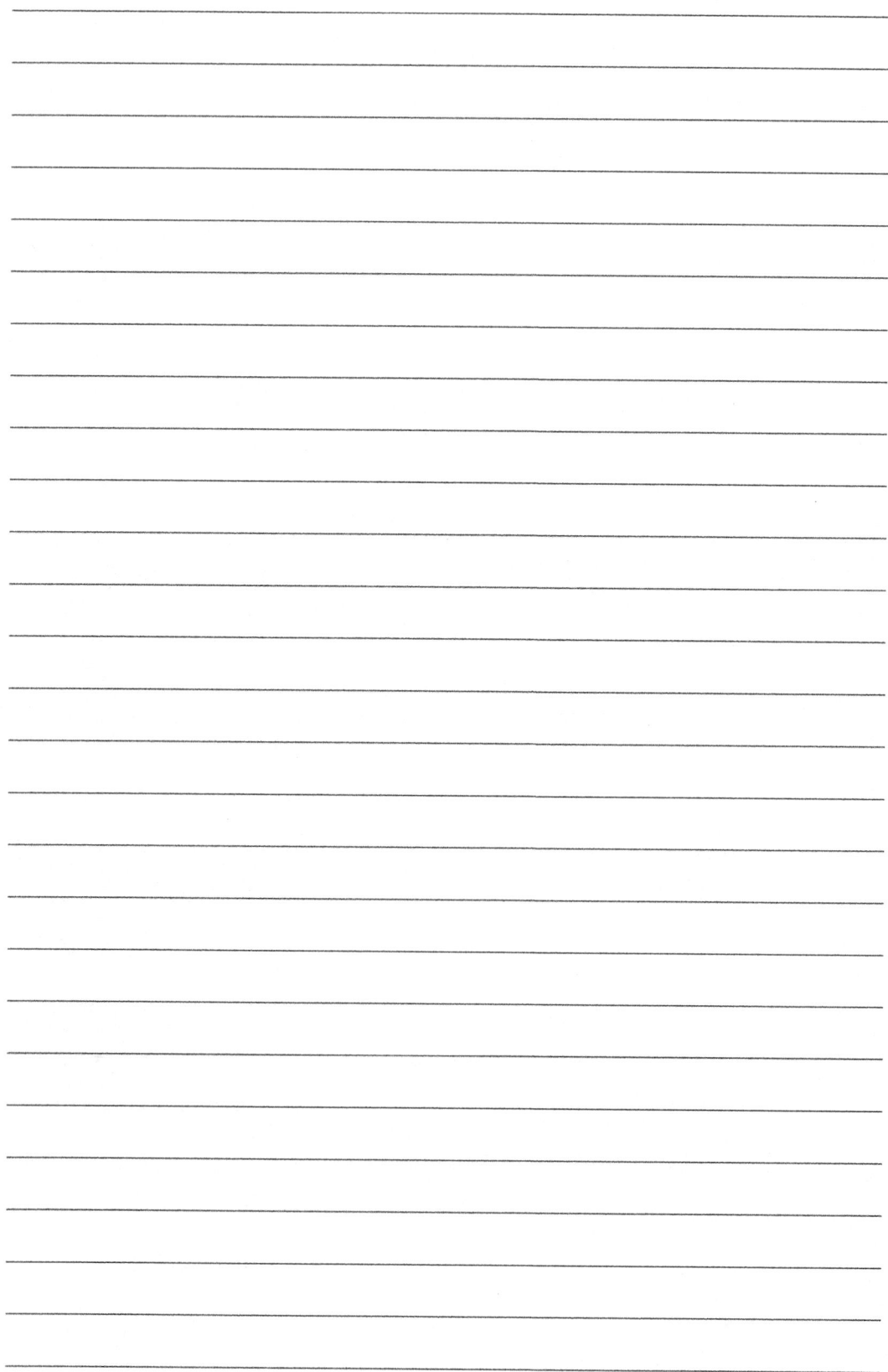

What faith did your parents and other relatives practice?

Share some funny family stories that happened during your childhood?

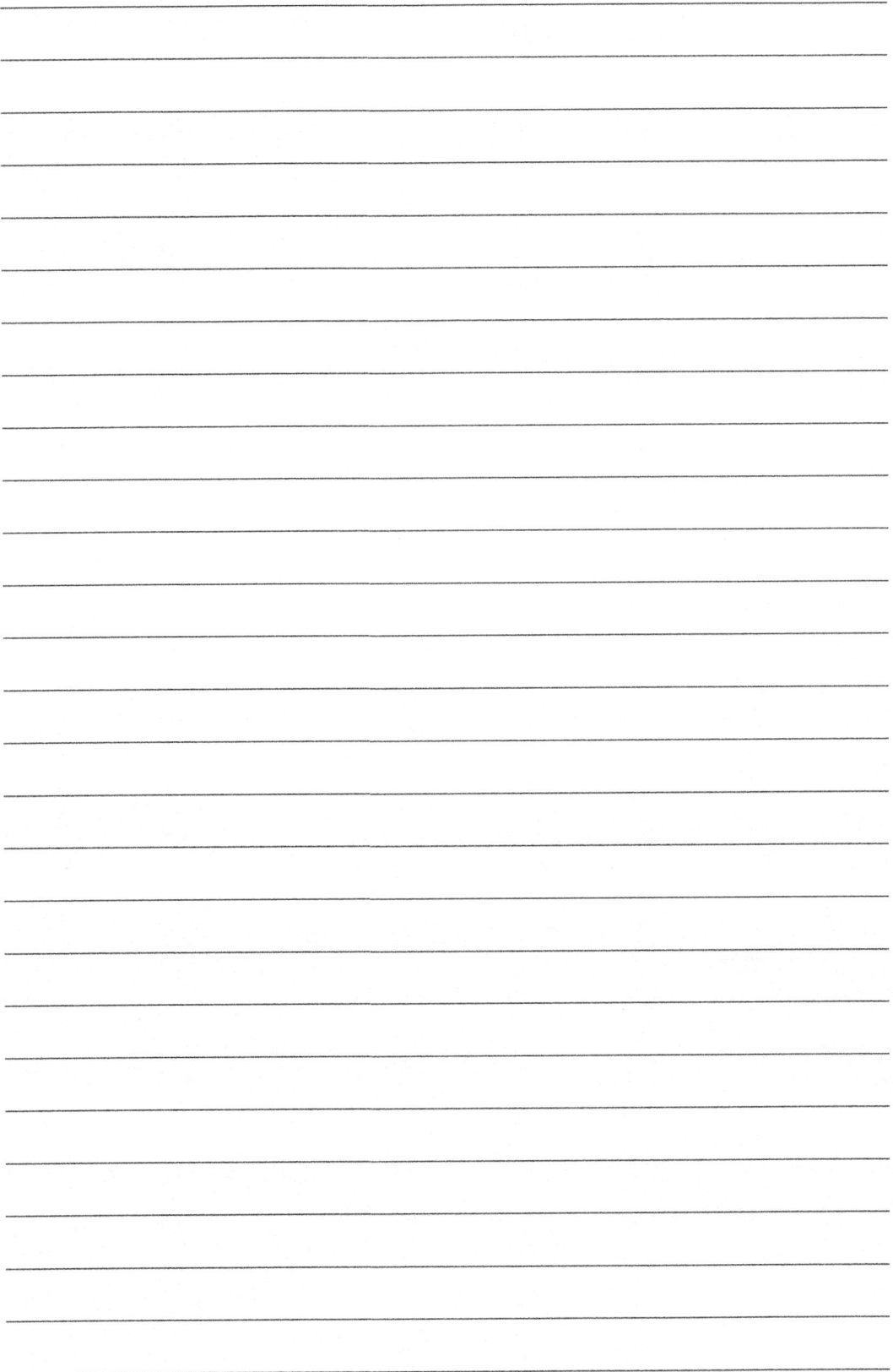

CHILDHOOD PHOTOS:
(INCLUDE DATES WHERE POSSIBLE)

CHILDHOOD PHOTOS:
(INCLUDE DATES WHERE POSSIBLE)

YOUNG ADULT

What did you do after high school?

_____

_____

_____

_____

_____

_____

_____

_____

_____

_____

_____

_____

_____

_____

_____

_____

_____

_____

_____

_____

_____

When did you get your first job and what was it? How did it go? What do you remember?

_____

_____

_____

_____

_____

_____

_____

_____

_____

_____

_____

_____

_____

_____

_____

_____

_____

_____

_____

What other jobs did you have? Share some thoughts about your favorite job as well as least favorite.

_____

_____

_____

_____

_____

_____

_____

_____

_____

_____

_____

What are some words you would use to describe your career?

_____

_____

_____

_____

_____

_____

_____

_____

Looking back on your young adult life, what are some of your regrets?

_____

_____

_____

_____

_____

_____

_____

_____

_____

_____

_____

_____

_____

_____

_____

_____

_____

_____

_____

_____

Looking back at your young adult life, what are you most proud of?

_____

_____

_____

_____

_____

_____

_____

_____

_____

_____

_____

_____

_____

_____

_____

_____

_____

_____

_____

_____

What was your greatest adventure as a young adult?

_____

_____

_____

_____

_____

_____

_____

_____

_____

Describe the funniest thing that's happened to you during your young adult days?

_____

_____

_____

_____

_____

_____

_____

_____

_____

Share about the mentors or people who influenced you as a young adult.

_____

_____

_____

_____

_____

_____

_____

_____

_____

_____

_____

_____

_____

_____

_____

_____

_____

_____

_____

_____

What did you believe as a young adult that you still believe today?

_____

_____

_____

_____

_____

_____

_____

What did you study or pursue as a young adult?

_____

_____

_____

_____

_____

_____

_____

_____

_____

ADULTHOOD/PARENT

Is love at first sight something you believe in?
Explain why you say yes or no?

_____

_____

_____

_____

_____

_____

_____

_____

_____

_____

_____

_____

_____

_____

_____

_____

_____

_____

_____

Who was your first romantic partner?
Describe your relationship?
How long did you date?

_____

_____

_____

_____

_____

_____

_____

_____

_____

_____

_____

_____

_____

_____

_____

_____

_____

_____

_____

_____

How and when did you meet your current partner?
Was it love at first sight?
What qualities did she/he have that you admired?

_____

_____

_____

_____

_____

_____

_____

_____

_____

_____

_____

_____

_____

_____

_____

_____

_____

_____

_____

_____

If married, describe the marriage proposal.
How did you know she/he was "the one" for you?

_____

_____

_____

_____

_____

_____

_____

_____

_____

_____

_____

_____

_____

_____

_____

_____

_____

_____

_____

_____

_____

Where and when was your wedding? Describe the ceremony and any other memories about that day?

Wedding Date:

Place:

_____

_____

_____

_____

_____

_____

_____

_____

_____

_____

_____

_____

_____

_____

_____

_____

_____

_____

What is the secret to a good marriage or relationship?

If married/if you were married, describe your in-laws? Include names and other interesting details.

As a parent, what were the most important traditions you've created for your family?

_____

_____

_____

_____

_____

_____

_____

_____

_____

_____

_____

_____

_____

_____

_____

_____

_____

_____

_____

_____

_____

In which ways did your views on marriage change over time?
What has your marriage taught you about relationships?

Share some of your favorite/memorable moments as a parent/grandparent?

_____

_____

_____

_____

_____

_____

_____

_____

_____

_____

_____

_____

_____

_____

_____

_____

_____

_____

_____

_____

_____

_____

_____

_____

_____

ADULTHOOD PHOTOS:
(INCLUDE DATES WHERE POSSIBLE)

ADULTHOOD PHOTOS:
(INCLUDE DATES WHERE POSSIBLE)

What lessons have you learned about parenting as you raised your children? What is the most rewarding thing about being a grand/parent?

_____

_____

_____

_____

_____

_____

_____

_____

_____

_____

_____

_____

_____

_____

_____

_____

_____

_____

_____

_____

_____

What are your hopes for your children / grandchildren?

What were/are your fears as an adult / parent / grandparent?

What has been/is the most fulfilling part of adulthood/being a parent?

_____

_____

_____

_____

_____

_____

_____

_____

_____

_____

_____

_____

_____

_____

_____

_____

_____

_____

_____

_____

_____

What was the most lonely time in your life?

_____

_____

_____

_____

_____

_____

_____

_____

What advice would you give to your 25 year old self today?

_____

_____

_____

_____

_____

_____

_____

_____

_____

_____

_____

If you could go back in time, what would you do more of or less of? Why?

What are some of the best investments (energy, time, money etc) you have made? Explain why?

_____

_____

_____

_____

_____

_____

_____

In the last few years, what new behaviour, habit or belief has most improved your life?

_____

_____

_____

_____

_____

_____

_____

_____

_____

_____

_____

_____

How is your relationship with your children/grandchildren today? What would you like to change? What are you happy with?

_____

_____

_____

_____

_____

_____

_____

_____

_____

_____

_____

_____

_____

_____

_____

_____

_____

_____

_____

_____

What do you enjoy most about growing older? What do you find less enjoyable as you age? Describe your most memorable moments as an adult?

Describe one of your worst moments as an adult?

What possessions/things do you cherish today?

Describe your lifelong friends. Include as much detail as possible about each person.

_____

_____

_____

_____

_____

_____

_____

_____

_____

_____

_____

_____

_____

_____

_____

_____

_____

_____

_____

_____

FAVORITES TODAY:

(extra space in case you have more favorites to share)

Movie:

Book:

Season:

Color:

Flavor of ice cream:

Flower:

Meal:

Animal:

Holiday:

Restaurant:

Places:

Game:

Sport:

Drink:

What were the hardest choices you ever had to make?

_____

_____

_____

_____

_____

_____

_____

Did anything or anyone change the course of your life?
Why/how?

_____

_____

_____

_____

_____

_____

_____

_____

_____

_____

_____

_____

As an adult, what prizes or awards have you won?
How did you win them?

_____

_____

_____

_____

_____

_____

_____

_____

Describe the most scenic place you've ever visited?
Which states/countries have you visited?

_____

_____

_____

_____

_____

_____

_____

_____

_____

_____

_____

_____

_____

What activities do you really enjoy as an adult?

_____

_____

_____

_____

_____

What are your hobbies?

_____

_____

_____

_____

_____

_____

What groups or organizations have you been a member of?

_____

_____

_____

_____

_____

_____

If given the chance, list a few places you'd like to visit.

_____

_____

_____

_____

_____

_____

What is something you've always wanted to do,
but never have?

_____

_____

_____

What's the easiest thing about being an adult?

_____

_____

_____

_____

_____

_____

_____

BRIEFLY...

Describe what you believe has been the greatest
invention of all time and why?

_____

_____

_____

_____

_____

Describe a moment in history that you'll never forget?

_____

_____

_____

_____

_____

What do you like about your generation?

_____

_____

_____

_____

What amazes you about life and society today?

_____

_____

_____

_____

Looking back, what are you the most proud of?

_____

_____

_____

What advice would you give your 5 year old self?

_____

_____

_____

What is your favorite part of yourself?

_____

_____

_____

What do you miss the most about the "old days"?

_____

_____

_____

What's a risk you took in life that you glad you did?

_____

_____

_____

_____

If you ruled the world for a day, what three things would you change or do?

_____

_____

_____

_____

_____

If you could wish for 3 things, what would you wish for?

_____

_____

_____

_____

What's the best gift you've ever received?

_____

_____

_____

_____

What are you most thankful for today?

_____

_____

_____

_____

_____

_____

Which mistakes taught you the most in life?
Describe the mistake and the lesson it taught you.

_____

_____

_____

_____

_____

_____

_____

_____

What are some things you wish you had done differently as a
parent/grandparent?

_____

_____

_____

_____

_____

_____

_____

_____

_____

_____

_____

_____

What are some things that you do
differently from your parents?

_____

_____

_____

_____

_____

_____

_____

_____

_____

What makes you feel loved?

_____

_____

_____

_____

_____

_____

_____

_____

_____

_____

What are your spiritual/religious traditions?
What is it like? What role do your beliefs play in your life
today? What would you tell your children/grandchildren
about your faith?

_____

_____

_____

_____

_____

_____

_____

_____

What has been the most joyous and
fulfilling times of your life?

_____

_____

_____

_____

_____

_____

_____

_____

_____

_____

_____

Describe a difficult time and the lesson it taught you.
What have your learned over your lifetime that you would like
to share with younger generations?

_____

_____

_____

_____

_____

_____

_____

_____

_____

_____

_____

_____

_____

_____

_____

_____

_____

_____

How do you define a good or successful life?

_____

_____

_____

_____

_____

_____

What's the best compliment you've received?

_____

_____

_____

_____

_____

What are your favorite conversation topics?

_____

_____

_____

_____

_____

_____

_____

_____

What's the first memory that springs to mind when you think back on....

Your first day at school:

_____

_____

Christmas or any holiday you loved:

_____

_____

Your first kiss:

_____

_____

Summers when you were a teen:

_____

_____

The morning of your first job as a young adult:

_____

_____

The birth of your first child:

_____

_____

_____

Your parents:

_____

_____

_____

Using technology for the first time:

_____

_____

Moving away from your childhood home:

_____

_____

7 DAY DIARY

Please share your feelings and thoughts over the course of 7 days. It doesn't have to be consecutive days. This will provide a fascinating glimpse into your life today.

Today's Date:

How are you feeling?

What are you thankful for today?

How did you spend your day?

Today's Date:

How are you feeling?

What are you thankful for today?

How did you spend your day?

Today's Date:

How are you feeling?

What are you thankful for today?

How did you spend your day?

Today's Date:

How are you feeling?

What are you thankful for today?

How did you spend your day?

Today's Date:

How are you feeling?

What are you thankful for today?

How did you spend your day?

Today's Date:

How are you feeling?

What are you thankful for today?

How did you spend your day?

Today's Date:

How are you feeling?

What are you thankful for today?

How did you spend your day?

Share some of your unique sayings / favorite quotes:

Use the next few pages for any other memories, stories or thoughts you would like to share.

Made in United States
North Haven, CT
03 April 2025

67508646R00059